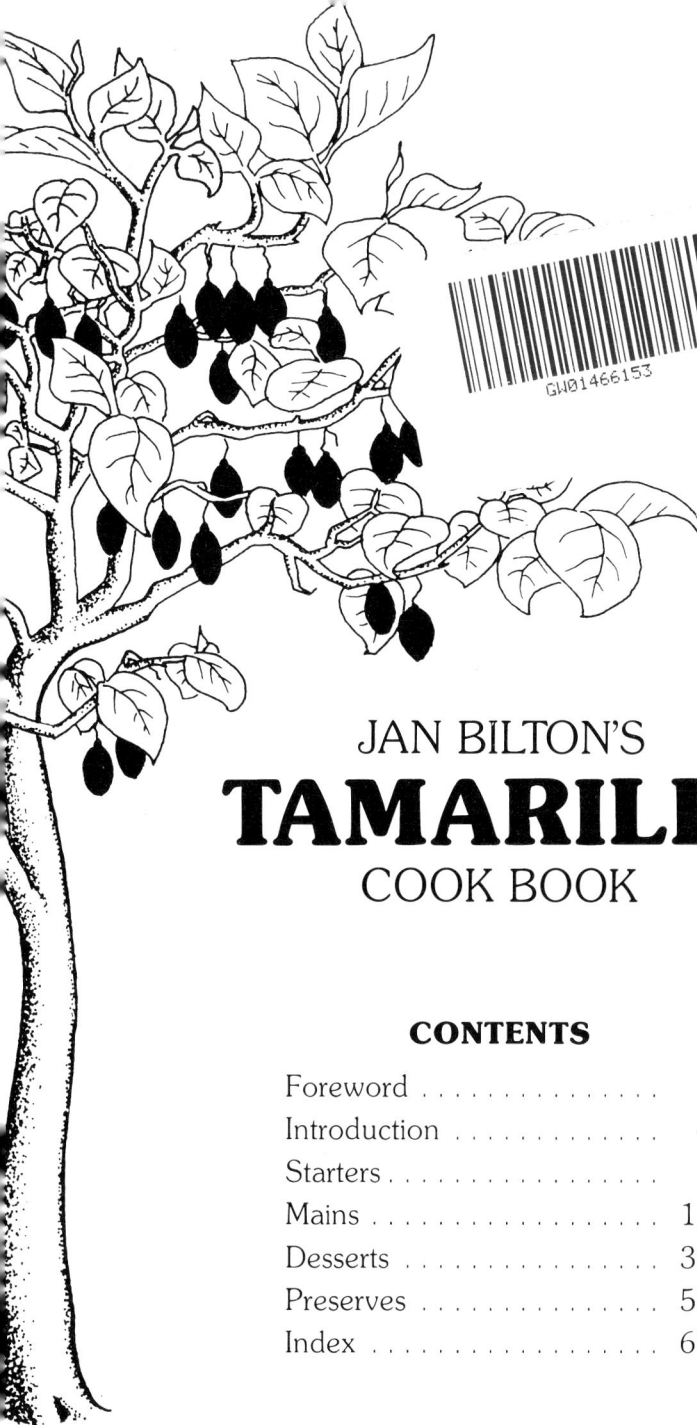

JAN BILTON'S

TAMARILLO
COOK BOOK

CONTENTS

Thank you Lorna Laurenson for your enthusiasm and encouragement.

ABOUT THE AUTHOR

Jan Bilton has been writing about food for 15 years. She finds her creative talents useful in developing new recipes and preparing food for photography. She has been the food editor for a large newspaper and written for magazines throughout the world. She is frequently heard on radio and seen on television. Her studies have been at the Home Science School of Otago University and at many cooking schools worldwide. *Jan Bilton's Tamarillo Cook Book* is the result of hours of testing and experimentation, and is her tenth book on food, many of which sell in Australia, USA, Japan and the UK.

Other books by the same author are —
New Zealand Kiwifruit Cook Book
New Zealand Microwave Cook Book
The Great New Zealand Cook Book
New Zealand Dinner Party Cook Book
Making the Most of Meat
Summer Food
Fresh and Fancy Fare

Publisher: Irvine Holt, P.O. Box 28019, Auckland 5, New Zealand.
Photography: Rees Osborne. Illustrations: Robert Bilton
Printing through Communication Arts
© Copyright 1986 Irvine Holt. ISBN 0-9597594-1-7
Overseas enquiries: NZ$7.95 plus $1 postage and handling per book, mail to publisher.

FOREWORD

The tamarillo is endemic to the Andes region of Central and South America and came to New Zealand rather circuitously via India in the early 1890s. Early plantings produced fruit ranging in colour from purple to yellow. Today the red variety is the most popular although there are increasing enquiries for the golden tamarillo.

The first known record of the tamarillo in New Zealand is in the 1891-92 catalogue of D. Hay & Sons, of Parnell, Auckland. The nursery had obtained some seed in autumn 1891 from the hill district of India, where the plant was growing wild.

It was not until World War II that tamarillos became a significant crop when the supplies of citrus from overseas were restricted. It was recognised that the tamarillo was a rich source of Vitamin C and so was grown as a substitute for citrus. The fruit has now been established to be high in carotene, Vitamins B and E and dietary fibre.

The tamarillo requires specialised growing conditions — well-drained soils, good shelter, humid atmosphere, little frost and good summer water. They are a challenge to grow.

But increasing interest in tamarillos from overseas encourages experimentation. The interest is sparked because of the adaptability of the fruit, the bold taste, bright colour and high nutritional value. In this book, Jan Bilton highlights the versatility of the fruit and demonstrates some exciting uses. She has also produced beautiful photographs to illustrate her theme. I hope you not only enjoy reading her recipes, but can savour them with good friends and company.

JOHN LAURENSON
Chairman
NZ Tamarillo Growers' Association

3

INTRODUCTION

THE SURPRISING TAMARILLO: Colourful, tasty, versatile and full of good health, the tamarillo is winning international acclaim. The unique flavour and brilliant colours open new possibilities for everyone who enjoys experimenting with food.

The flesh of the red tamarillo has been likened to the exotic pomegranate in look, but the taste of either the red or yellow variety, cannot be compared to any other fruit. The distinctive, tangy flavour complements both sweet and savoury foods.

THE TREE: The tamarillo grows on a tree which reaches about 4 metres (12 feet) in height. The tree has large heart-shaped leaves and brittle branches. The oval fruits, about the size of large eggs, hang in clusters and come in a variety of colours from red to gold. They ripen during the winter season — in New Zealand from May to September.

THE FRUIT: Inside the red tamarillo, the golden flesh is dotted with red seeds. The gold-skinned variety has a similar seed structure but is totally gold throughout. The seeds and flesh of both are edible, the skin has an astringent taste and is not usually eaten. The flavour of the red variety is more pronounced, the golden being the sweeter of the two.

THE NAME: The name 'tamarillo' is derived from the Spanish word *amarillo*, meaning yellow. The original name of tree tomato was discarded in 1967 to avoid confusion on the export market. The tamarillo does have a similar seed structure to the tomato and it looks like an elongated one, but there the similarity stops. The terrific taste of tamarillos allows them to be used with sweet and savoury foods in dozens of different ways.

NUTRITIONAL VALUE: All varieties of tamarillo are high in Vitamins A and E as well as Vitamins B and C — 31 mg of Vitamin C per 100 g (3½ oz) fruit. Tamarillos are also a good supply of minerals — phosphorus 39 mg per 100 g (3½ oz) fruit; potassium 321 mg per 100 g (3½ oz) fruit. They are low in kilojoules (calories), about 109 kJ (26 calories) per 100g (3½ oz) of fruit.

STORAGE: Ripe fruit are firm to feel but the stems turn from green to yellow and the calyx at the base starts to curl. Store ripened fruit in a plastic bag in the refrigerator or in the crisper bin, for up to 3 weeks. For longer storage they should be deep frozen or preserved (see page 57).

EATING: The tamarillo can be eaten directly from its natural shell, by cutting in half and scooping out the flesh with a spoon. The raw fruit can be sweetened with white or brown sugar before eating. The fruit may also be cooked or puréed, but because of the high acidity always use ceramic, enamel or stainless saucepans to avoid discolouring.

PEELING: The tamarillo may be peeled using a sharp knife, but the skin is removed more easily if the fruit is blanched first. Remove the stalks, place the fruit in a bowl, then cover with boiling water. Stand for 2 minutes then drain. Refresh fruit in cold water for 2 minutes, then peel off the skin.

All recipes in this book use standard level measurements.

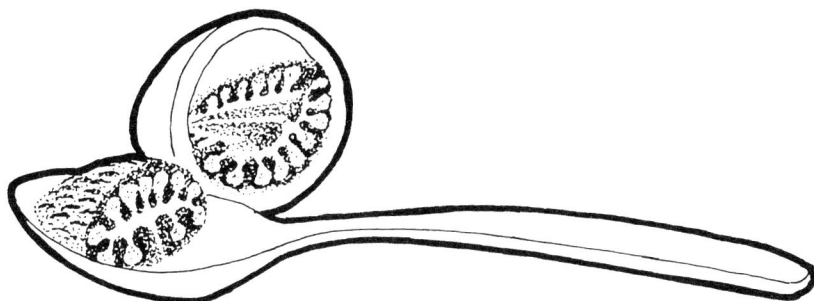

STARTERS

Snacks, sandwiches, drinks, salads and light meals.

Platter Foods

Suggested toppings for canapés:
* square bread croûtons topped with sliced tamarillo and caviar (see photograph page 9)
* crackers with sliced tamarillo glazed with aspic and topped with shrimps and dill
* heart-shaped rye bread croûtons, topped with tamarillo and piped with salmon paté
* tamarillos and raw diced mushrooms filled into crisp vol au vents
* quartered, peeled tamarillos wrapped in strips of prosciutto or ham
* mini taco shells filled with lettuce and cheese and topped with chilli flavoured tamarillo purée

Sandwiches

* smoked eel and sliced tamarillo with alfalfa sprouts in rye
* open sandwich of shredded lettuce, tamarillo and sliced avocado topped with crisp onion rings
* hot beef on rye with rich brown gravy and halved tamarillos
* pita bread sandwich of bean sprouts, quartered tamarillos and cottage cheese
* B.L.T. — bacon, lettuce and tamarillo sandwich prepared from toasted bread
* croissants filled with salami, tamarillo and watercress

Fancy French Toast

1 ¼ cups cream
3 eggs
1 loaf French bread
juice of 1 orange
2 tablespoons honey
3 tablespoons brandy
6 large tamarillos, peeled
6 rashers bacon

Whisk cream and eggs well. Slice bread into 2.5 cm (1 in) rounds and arrange in a single layer in a wide, shallow casserole. Pour egg over bread to cover evenly. Refrigerate overnight or several hours.

Heat juice, honey and brandy until warm. Cut tamarillos in half lengthwise. Add to juice mixture and stand on a warm element to heat through.

Panfry bacon until crisp. Remove to a warm platter. Fry rounds of bread in bacon fat until golden on both sides. Add a little butter if bread begins to stick. Divide bread and bacon onto 6 serving plates and spoon on some of the fruit sauce. Serve immediately for breakfast, brunch or lunch.

Seafood Dip

(see photograph page 21)

Purée 6 raw, peeled tamarillos. Season with a dash of salt, some pepper and ½ teaspoon sugar. Finely chop 2 shallots and add with 2 tablespoons olive oil. Use as a dip for prawns or wontons.

DRINKS

Tamarillos can be puréed and mixed with a variety of splits or other juices. Purée either the raw peeled fruit or cooked fruit. Cooked fruit blends well with milk drinks — combine with yoghurt or ice cream, a little honey to sweeten and blend well. Four tamarillos yield about 1 cup purée. This may be stored in the refrigerator for several days or in the deep freeze.

Tamarillo Coolers

4 tamarillos
2-3 teaspoons sugar
tonic or mineral water

Halve tamarillos and scoop out as much flesh as possible. Purée in a blender or food processor or pass through a sieve. Mix with sugar to taste.

Fill 3 or 4 glasses with ice, pour over some purée and top up with chilled tonic water or mineral water. Add a dash of gin or vodka for extra zing.

Traffic Lights

2 red tamarillos
2 golden tamarillos
2 kiwifruit
sugar to taste

Peel and purée fruit separately. Sweeten according to taste. Chill.

Pour kiwifruit in to the base of 2-3 glasses. Carefully spoon over the golden purée, then top with the red. If desired, each purée may be flavoured with a liqueur. For example, crème de menthe with kiwifruit, orange curaçao with the golden tamarillo and cherry brandy with the red.

Moulded Beet and Tamarillo Salad

450 g (1 lb) can beetroot
4 red tamarillos, peeled and sliced
3 teaspoons powdered gelatine
½ cup hot water
1 teaspoon sugar
2 tablespoons vinegar

Strain the beetroot retaining the liquid. Slice beetroot into strips and place alternately into a mould with the tamarillo (or prepare 6 individual moulds).

Soak gelatine in a little beetroot juice until swollen. Dissolve in the boiling water. Add to remaining juice with sugar and vinegar. If necessary, make up to 1½ cups with a little water or red wine. Refrigerate until syrupy then pour over the mixture in the mould. Refrigerate until firm.

Unmould onto crisp lettuce leaves and garnish with small flowers. Good served with the Tamarillo Mayonnaise.

Salad Ideas

Tamarillos provide tang, colour and flavour to many salad combinations. It is usually best to add them at the last minute to prevent their bright colour from discolouring other ingredients.

- sliced mushrooms and sliced tamarillos, tossed with vinaigrette
- shredded red cabbage, tamarillo and apple slaw
- tamarillo and avocado salad
- shredded carrot, diced celery, raisins and tamarillos
- broccoli flowerettes, blanched and chilled, served on a lettuce cup with quartered tamarillos and a cream dressing
- tossed green salad with tamarillo vinaigrette — to make, add a chopped tamarillo to a good French dressing.

Sunset Salad

A crunchy treat

2 cups cracked wheat
1 cup boiling water
2 tamarillos
1 medium onion, diced finely
¾ cup chopped parsley
¼ cup chopped mint
½ cup lemon juice
salt
freshly ground black pepper

Soak the cracked wheat in boiling water for 1 hour. Drain.

Peel and dice the tamarillos. Combine with onion, parsley and mint and stir into the wheat. Combine juice and oil and stir enough into the salad to moisten well. Season with salt and pepper. Refrigerate 1 hour before serving. Serves 6.

Tamarillo Mayonnaise

This dressing is delicious! And easy to make.

1 red tamarillo, peeled
½ cup salad oil

Place the tamarillo into a blender or food processor and purée until smooth. With the motor running, slowly drizzle in the oil and mix until thick, like whipped cream.

Serve this tasty pink mayonnaise on halved avocados, potato salads, or use as a topping for seafoods or crisp fried chicken.

Chilled Tamarillo Soup

A delicious start to dinner (see photograph, page 33).

6 tamarillos, peeled
⅔ cup sugar
4 cups water
4 whole cloves
1 cinnamon stick
peel of 1 lemon
1 cup good red wine
2 tablespoons cornflour
juice of half a lemon

Place tamarillos in a saucepan with sugar, water, cloves, cinnamon stick and lemon peel. Bring to the boil, stirring gently. Poach for 10 minutes. Cool. Remove spices and lemon peel. Purée the fruit, sieve if desired, and place back into the saucepan. Bring to boiling point. Combine wine and cornflour and stir into the soup. Cook gently until mixture thickens, stirring constantly. Stir in lemon juice and chill. Serve garnished with herbs or flowers. Serves 4-6.

Spicy Winter Soup

25 g (1 oz) butter
1 medium onion, sliced
¼ cup brandy
1 teaspoon curry powder
4 tamarillos, peeled and diced
1 apple, peeled and diced
1 tablespoon sugar
salt and pepper
bouquet garni
2½ cups beef or chicken stock

Melt butter in a heavy saucepan and sauté onion until transparent. Add brandy, warm slightly then flame. Stir in curry powder and cook 1 minute. Add all other ingredients. Cover and simmer for 30 minutes. Discard bouquet garni and purée. Serve topped with cream and crisp bread croûtons. Serves 4.

Bougainville Surprise

½ a medium red cabbage
3 tamarillos, peeled
½ cup sultanas
½ cup currants
50 g (2 oz) butter
3 tablespoons red wine vinegar
2 teaspoons sugar
1 tablespoon mustard seeds
¼ teaspoon caraway seeds
salt and pepper

Shred cabbage finely, removing any thick ribs. Wash well under the cold water tap. Drain. Melt butter in a saucepan and add sliced tamarillos, sultanas and currants. Cook for 3 minutes on low heat. Add cabbage and cook for 5 minutes, stirring. Add vinegar and sugar. Cover and simmer gently for 30 minutes. When cabbage is cooked, stir in mustard and caraway seeds and season with salt and pepper. Serve with main course meals. Serves 6.

Sweet Golden Potatoes

500 g (1 lb) kumara or sweet potato
4 golden tamarillos, peeled
3 tablespoons brown sugar
1 tablespoon lemon juice
freshly grated nutmeg
50 g (2 oz) butter
¼ cup chopped walnuts

Peel and boil the sweet potato until just cooked. Drain well. Slice into 5 mm (¼ in) rounds. Arrange in a 23 cm (9 in) baking dish. Slice tamarillos and place over the potato. Sprinkle with sugar, juice and nutmeg. Dot with butter and walnuts. Bake, uncovered at 190°C (375°F) for 35 minutes. Serves about 6.

Keri Lasagne with Mushrooms and Ham

2 sheets fresh lasagne
500 g (1 lb) cottage cheese
¼ cup cream
1 egg
salt and pepper
150 g (5 oz) mushrooms
1 large onion, diced
25 g (1 oz) butter
4 tamarillos
125 g (4 oz) ham, chopped
2 tablespoons finely chopped parsley
½ teaspoon dried basil
2 tablespoons white wine
1 cup grated Cheddar cheese

Trim pasta to fit a 20 cm (8 in) square baking dish. Lightly grease the dish and place a layer of pasta in the base.

Combine cottage cheese with cream, egg, salt and pepper.

Slice mushrooms and sauté in butter with onion until soft.

Peel and chop tamarillos. Add to mushrooms with ham, parsley, basil and wine. Bring to the boil, reduce heat then simmer, uncovered for 5 minutes.

Spread one half of the cottage cheese mixture onto the pasta in the baking dish, then cover with one half of the tamarillo mixture and half the Cheddar cheese. Top with more pasta and repeat the layers.

Cover and bake 180°C (350°F) for 35-40 minutes.
Serves 4.

Fondue Honore

A tasty cheese fondue which is lightened with the addition of tamarillos.

15 g (½ oz) butter
1 medium onion, diced
4 red tamarillos, peeled
500 g (1 lb) shredded Cheddar cheese
1 cup milk, scalded

In the top part of the double boiler, melt the butter and sauté the onion and chopped tamarillos until soft.

Place the saucepan over boiling water and gradually stir in the cheese. When beginning to melt, slowly pour in the hot milk, stirring well.

Pour the mixture into a fondue pot or chafing dish and keep warm.

Serve with chunks of French bread and taco chips. Use these as dippers for the fondue. Accompany with a crisp salad. Serves 4.

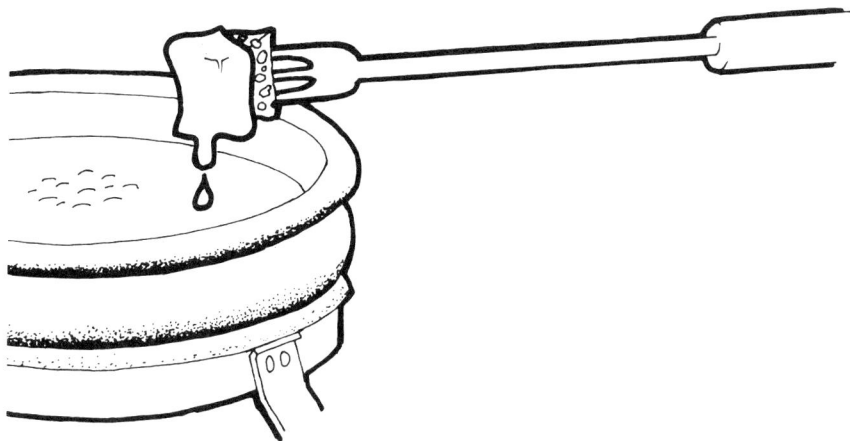

Marinated Brie with Tamarillo and Basil

A tasty light lunch or starter to dinner. Mozzarella could be used in place of the Brie.

125 g (4 oz) Brie
3 tablespoons mild olive oil
2 tablespoons salad oil
1 clove garlic, crushed
1 tablespoon finely chopped fresh basil
1 tablespoon finely chopped fresh parsley
salt
freshly ground black pepper
2 tamarillos
fresh herbs for garnish

Slice Brie thinly and layer on a serving plate.

Whisk oils, garlic, basil and parsley until well combined. Sprinkle over the cheese and marinate at room temperature for 2 hours.

Peel and slice tamarillos and layer on plate in an attractive pattern. Sprinkle with salt and pepper, a little of the dressing and garnish with herbs. Serves 2.

Stilton Starter

Arrange a platter of Stilton cheese and tamarillos, peeled and quartered lengthwise. Serve with thin rye biscuits and lightly chilled glasses of claret.

MAINS

The colour and flavour of tamarillos make intriguing additions to main courses.

Steaks and chops can be topped with slices of peeled or unpeeled tamarillos which add eye-appeal and complementary flavour.

As an accompaniment to curries, the fruit can be peeled and diced and served as a side dish or combined with plain yoghurt to serve as a rayta.

Casseroles benefit from the tangy flavour of the fruit and tamarillos can also be added to stuffings for poultry, lamb, pork or fish.

Tamarillos can be fried with onions to serve with main courses, and they make attractive edible garnishes also. Slice the fruit and stem in half lengthwise, and place on the serving plate with sprigs of fresh herbs.

As a marinade, the puréed fruit gives colour, flavour and helps to tenderise. Combine the purée with your favourite herbs and spices and use as a barbecue accompaniment.

Cooked or raw, the tamarillo is terrific!

Timbale of Seafood with Tamarillo Hollandaise

Choose firm white fish or salmon or a selection of shellfish (e.g. scallops) and fish

500 g (1 lb) fresh fillets of fish
¼ cup sour cream
2 eggs, separated
¼ teaspoon salt
⅛ teaspoon white pepper
1 tablespoon horseradish cream
1 cup cream, whipped

Tamarillo Hollandaise
2 red tamarillos
1 tablespoon lemon juice
3 egg yolks
150 g (5 oz) clarified butter

Discard any skin or bones from the fish. Slice, then place in a food processor or blender and purée. Place in a bowl.

Combine sour cream with egg yolks and heat over low heat until slightly thick. Add to the fish with seasonings and horseradish cream. Beat egg whites until stiff. Fold whipped cream and whites into the fish.

Lightly grease a 23 cm (9 in) ring mould. Pour fish mixture into the mould and place in a baking pan of hot water. The water should come up to the level of the fish in the ring mould. Bake 30 minutes at 180°C (350°F).

Meanwhile, prepare the hollandaise. Peel and chop the two tamarillos. Simmer on low heat until cooked. Add lemon juice then purée in a food processor. Sieve if desired. Add egg yolks and mix well.

Melt butter over low heat. With processor motor running, slowly pour in the butter, beating until thick. Keep sauce warm over a bowl of hot water. When fish is cooked, remove from oven and invert mould onto a serving plate. Pour Tamarillo Hollandaise around base of the fish and serve immediately. Serves 4.

Hapuka in Spicy Tamarillo Sauce

A saucy fish dish.

4 × 225 g (8 oz) hapuka (groper) steaks
1 teaspoon salt
1 tablespoon lemon juice
3 red tamarillos
1 medium onion, minced
1 clove garlic, crushed
3 tablespoons olive oil
1 teaspoon sugar
¼ cup finely chopped parsley
3 tablespoons tomato paste
¾ cup dry sherry
¼ cup water
4 slices lemon
50 g (2 oz) butter
4 slices tamarillo
sprigs of dill or fennel

Place hapuka in an oiled shallow baking dish and sprinkle with salt and lemon juice.

Peel and slice the 3 tamarillos. Place in a saucepan with onion, garlic and olive oil and simmer until soft. Add sugar, parsley and tomato paste.

Bring sherry to the boil in another saucepan and simmer for 2 minutes. Stir into tamarillo mixture and simmer until well blended.

Pour sauce over the fish in the pan. Top with lemon slices and dot with butter. Cover lightly with foil. Bake at 190°C (375°F) for about 40 minutes. Serve steaks topped with sauce and the tamarillo slices and herbs. Serves 4.

Spanish Salad with Crayfish

1 crayfish or lobster
1 medium onion
1 small green cucumber
1 green pepper
3 red tamarillos
salt and pepper
Caper Dressing
¼ cup mayonnaise
¼ cup sour cream
1 tablespoon capers
dash cayenne pepper

To prepare crayfish from the live state, immerse the fish in a large tub of cold water for about 2 hours. This will drown it. Place the crayfish in a saucepan of cold water and slowly bring to boiling point.

Poach until the fish shell has turned red. Remove from the pan and cool. Refrigerate until required.

Using a heavy knife, cut the crayfish in half through the centre from the head to the tail. Clean head area by washing under the cold water tap. Drain. Scoop out the flesh and cut into cubes. Replace back into the shells.

Dice onion and stand in icy water for 30 minutes. Drain. Dice pepper discarding the seeds. Halve cucumber and scoop out seeds with a teaspoon. Cut cucumber into similar sized dice.

Peel 2 tamarillos and dice. Sprinkle with salt and pepper. Place diced pepper, tamarillo and cucumber into the top portion of the crayfish, keeping each vegetable separate.

Place crayfish on a serving platter and surround with suitable green salad leaves. Place diced onion on top. Cut remaining tamarillo in a zig-zag fashion through the centre, then pull apart. Place on platter for a garnish.

Combine all ingredients for dressing. Serve separately. Serves 2-3.

Peppy Veal Paprika

2 tablespoons oil
2 onions, diced
1 kg (2 lb) stewing veal
2 tablespoons flour
⅛ teaspoon cayenne pepper
2 tamarillos, peeled and chopped
1 tablespoon paprika
125 g (4 oz) mushrooms, sliced
1 cup sour cream
¼ cup water
5 cups hot boiled rice
sliced tamarillos
mint leaves

Heat oil in a frypan and sauté onion until golden. Place in a casserole. Cut meat into 2.5 cm (1 in) cubes and panfry in batches until coloured. Place in casserole with onion.

Stir flour into the pan and add pepper, tamarillos, paprika, mushrooms and sour cream. Cook, stirring, over low heat for 1-2 minutes. Pour over the meat adding water if too thick. Cover and cook at 160°C (325°F) for 1½ hours until meat is tender.

To serve, pack the hot boiled rice into a lightly greased ring mould. Invert onto a serving dish and tap sharply to release rice onto the plate. Remove ring mould. Spoon veal into the centre. Surround rice around the outside with slices of peeled tamarillos and sprigs of mint. Serves 4-6.

Tamarillo Bourguignonne

A rich stew of beef, red wine and whole tamarillos.

1 kg (2 lb) lean beef for stewing
2 cups red wine
250 g (9 oz) bacon, chopped
25 g (1 oz) butter
8 shallots
2 tablespoons flour
1 teaspoon salt
4 peppercorns
1 bayleaf
½ cup water
2 tablespoons brown sugar
6 tamarillos
chopped parsley

Cut beef into 2.5 cm (1 in) cubes and place in a bowl. Pour the red wine over the meat and marinate overnight, turning occasionally. Drain and reserve the wine. Pat meat dry.

Sauté the chopped bacon in melted butter until crisp. Add peeled shallots and sauté 2 minutes. Place in a casserole. Sprinkle beef with flour and sauté in batches in the pan, until coloured. Place in the casserole also with seasonings. Add red wine, water and sugar to frypan and bring to the boil, scraping burnt pieces from the pan. Pour into the casserole. Cover and bake at 160°C (325°F) for 1½ hours.

Peel tamarillos leaving whole and with stalks on. Add to the casserole with a little more hot wine and water if necessary. Continue cooking for 30 minutes until tamarillos are tender. Serve in individual casseroles, with tamarillos on top, garnished with parsley. Serves 4-6.

Dressed Fillet of Beef on Croûton

2 kg (4 lb) fillet of beef
2 cloves garlic
50 g (2 oz) softened butter
tamarillo jelly (page 59)
or red currant jelly
bread
2 red tamarillos
2 golden tamarillos
6-8 lettuce leaves and/or curly kale
250 g (8 oz) snow peas

Fold over thin ends of the fillet to make it equal in thickness.
Secure with string. Peel garlic and cut cloves into slivers. With
the point of a sharp knife make small incisions in the beef and
insert the garlic. Spread generously with butter.

Place meat on a rack in a roasting pan. Preheat oven to
230°C (450°F). Place pan into the oven then reduce the
temperature to 180°C (350°F) for 30 minutes. Brush with
warmed jelly. Meat can be served hot on the croûton with hot
vegetables and tamarillos. The dish can also be served cold —
proceed as follows.

To make croûton, cut a slice of bread the length of the loaf,
about 2 cm (¾ in) thick. Brush with melted butter, and bake
in the oven at 180°C (350°F) for about 10 minutes until
crisp. Place on a serving plate.

Peel the tamarillos. Slice 1 red and 1 golden tamarillo
lengthwise, every 5 mm (¼ in), from tip almost to the stalk
end. Spread into a fan shape. Slice remaining fruit into
rounds.

Blanch curly kale, then the snow peas, for 1 minute in boiling
water. Refresh in icy water. Pat dry. Place meat on the
croûton on a serving platter. Surround with lettuce and kale,
the peas and tamarillos. Brush meat with more jelly and top
with sliced tamarillos. Serves about 8.

Pork Chops with Prunes and Tamarillos

Sauce
1 carrot
1 onion
1 stalk celery
25 g (1 oz) butter
1 bouquet garni
1 clove
salt and pepper
2 tablespoons red wine vinegar
1 cup Burgundy

8 prunes
4 tamarillos
2 tablespoons brown sugar
4 pork chops
1 tablespoon oil
50 g (2 oz) butter
1 tablespoon softened butter
1 tablespoon flour
chopped parsley

First prepare the sauce by dicing vegetables and sautéing in the 25 g (1 oz) butter with bouquet garni, clove, salt and pepper. When golden, add vinegar and wine and simmer for 20 minutes. Strain.

Meanwhile, cover prunes in water and cook for about 20 minutes, until plumped. Drain. Peel tamarillos leaving stalks on and poach in water to cover, adding the brown sugar. When just cooked, drain.

Melt the oil and 50 g (2 oz) butter in a heavy frypan and sauté chops about 6 minutes on both sides, seasoning with salt and pepper. When cooked and golden, remove and keep warm.

Work the softened butter and flour together and gradually whisk into the sauce. Add prunes and tamarillos and heat through. To serve, arrange chops on a plate, pour the sauce and fruit over and sprinkle with chopped parsley. Serves 4.

Saucy Lamb Kebabs with Peaches

A rich spicy sauce of tamarillos is used as a marinade for skewered lamb. The mild taste of peaches blends well with the combination.

6 tamarillos, peeled
¼ cup water
¼ cup sugar
1 tablespoon soy sauce
½ teaspoon Worcestershire sauce
½ teaspoon dried basil
1 clove garlic, crushed
1 kg (2 lb) lean lamb
8 cooked peach halves
25 g (1 oz) butter
salt and pepper

Slice tamarillos into water and sugar in a saucepan and bring to the boil. Cook until tender. Place in a blender or food processor with soy sauce, Worcestershire, basil and garlic. Blend until smooth.

Cut lamb into 2.5 cm (1 in) cubes. Thread onto skewers and place in a flat dish. Pour the cooled marinade over the meat. Marinate several hours, turning occasionally.

Drain skewers, place under a pre-heated grill and cook for about 4 minutes. Turn skewers and baste with marinade. Place peach halves on the rack beside the skewers, dot with butter and sprinkle with salt and pepper. Cook for a further 4 minutes. Serve with the warmed marinade. Serves 4.

Golden Rack of Lamb with Basil Meringue

Choose 4 racks of lamb of 4-6 cutlets each.

Golden sauce
4 golden tamarillos
¼ cup white wine
3 tablespoons sugar
¼ teaspoon salt
1 tablespoon orange flavoured liqueur

4 racks of lamb, skin removed
25 g (1 oz) butter
salt and pepper
2 egg whites
2 tablespoons finely chopped fresh basil
1 tablespoon finely chopped parsley
2 tamarillos

To prepare the sauce, peel tamarillos then slice into a food processor. Purée until smooth. Place in a saucepan with wine, sugar and salt and heat gently until sugar is dissolved. Just before serving add the liqueur.

Score fat on the lamb racks as you would a ham. Brush with melted butter and season with salt and pepper. Place meat in a baking dish fat side up. Bake 35 minutes at 200°C (400°F).

Beat egg whites until stiff. Carefully fold in finely chopped herbs. Spread mixture over the racks of lamb. Place under a hot grill until egg is set, about 3 minutes.

Place lamb on serving dishes with some golden sauce. Cut the two tamarillos in half lengthwise and use as an edible garnish. Serves 4.

Venison Steaks with Tamarillo Coulis

Venison cuts are similar to those of beef. Choose steaks about 2 cm (¾ in) thick.

Tamarillo Coulis
4 tamarillos
2 tablespoons lemon juice
¼ cup water
4 juniper berries
2 tablespoons sugar
2 tablespoons gin

500 g (1 lb) venison frying steaks
25 g (1 oz) butter
1 clove garlic, crushed
sliced tamarillo
watercress

To prepare the coulis, peel tamarillos and slice into a saucepan with lemon juice, water, juniper berries and sugar. Poach until just cooked, cover and allow to cool. Remove berries. Purée the mixture and sieve. Stir in the gin.

Trim steak and cut into serving sized pieces. Melt butter in a heavy frypan and add garlic. Fry steaks about 2-3 minutes each side until just cooked and still a little pink in the centre.

Warm the coulis slightly and place a little on each of 4 serving plates. Top with the steaks, slices of raw tamarillo (unpeeled), and sprigs of watercress. Serves 4.

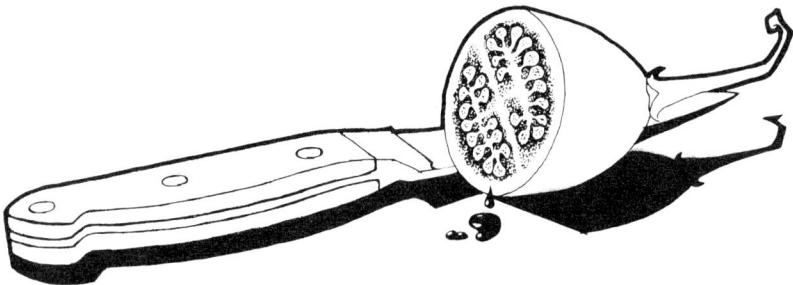

Exotic Braised Duck

1.5 kg (3 lb) duck
1 each onion, carrot, parsnip
bouquet garni
4 tablespoons wine vinegar
2 tablespoons sugar
½ cup port
6 tamarillos, peeled

Prepare duck for cooking. Place chopped onion, carrot and parsnip on the base of a heavy casserole. Place duck on top with bouquet garni and half cover with hot water. Cover casserole and either simmer gently on element for 1½ hours or in oven 180°C (350°F). Turn duck half way through cooking. Strain and reserve stock, skimming off any fat.

Meanwhile prepare sauce. Combine vinegar and sugar and simmer until sugar is lightly caramelised. Add port and 1 cup strained cooking stock and tamarillos. Simmer until tamarillos are tender. Purée and sieve. Reheat gently.

Remove meat from the duck and layer onto a serving plate or replace on carcass in original position. Pour the sauce over and serve immediately. Serves 4.

Chinese Chicken Wings

Peel and cut up 3 tamarillos. Place in a blender or food processor and purée until smooth. Combine with ¼ cup each, soy sauce, sugar, dry sherry, 1 tablespoon finely chopped root ginger, 1 teaspoon salt and some freshly ground black pepper. Pour over 1.75 kg (3½ lb) chicken wings and marinate several hours in the refrigerator. Drain chicken, reserving the marinade. Place chicken in a foil-lined oven pan. Bake 190°C (375°F) for about 35 minutes until cooked, basting occasionally with reserved marinade. Serve hot or cold. A good finger food or serve as a main course for 6.

Poussin with Compote of Tamarillo

Poussins are small chickens — one per person is usually served.

6 small poussins, weighing about 400 g (14 oz) each
½ cup seasoned flour
2 eggs, lightly beaten
½ cup milk
1½ cups toasted breadcrumbs
25 g (1 oz) butter, melted
6 large red tamarillos
1½ cups medium white wine
¼ cup sugar
2 tablespoons cider vinegar
1 cinnamon stick
4 cloves
3 whole allspice

Wipe poussins dry. Tie legs together or secure with skewers. Toss in flour, brush with eggs combined with milk, coat in breadcrumbs. Press in well then refrigerate to set coating, about 1 hour.

Lightly grease a large baking pan. Place poussins in and bake at 180°C (350°F) for 1 hour.

Peel tamarillos, leaving the stalks intact. Heat wine, sugar and vinegar in a wide saucepan, stirring until sugar is dissolved. Add spices and simmer for 10 minutes. Place tamarillos into the saucepan and poach 3-4 minutes.

To serve, slice each tamarillo into quarters leaving stalk end intact. Place beside chickens on serving plates. Garnish with spring onion curls. Serves 6.

Chicken Schnitzel, Rosé Sauce and Pink Peppercorns

Try this sauce recipe with veal also.

2 large tamarillos, peeled
1 cup rosé wine
1 cup cream
2 tablespoons pink peppercorns
500 g (1 lb) chicken schnitzel
1 tablespoon oil
25 g (1 oz) butter
fresh tarragon for garnishing

Place tamarillos in a saucepan with the wine and poach until tender. Purée and sieve. Simmer mixture gently for 5 minutes.

Meanwhile snip schnitzel around the outside edge to prevent it curling during cooking. Melt oil and butter in a frypan, then sauté the chicken about 2 minutes each side. Remove to a warm serving platter. Wipe pan clean with a paper towel.

Pour in tamarillo and wine mixture, then stir in the cream. Cook until slightly thickened. Rinse and drain peppercorns and add to the sauce. Spoon over the schnitzels. Garnish with tarragon. Serves 4.

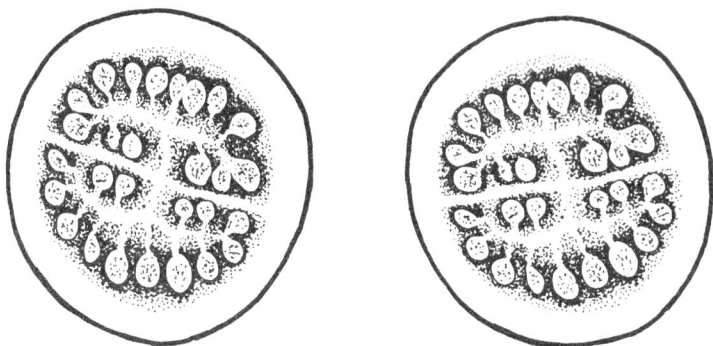

DESSERTS

The tamarillo is a versatile ending to dinner. It may be eaten fresh or poached. Peeled and sliced, it can be served sweetened with a little honey or maple syrup, and topped with yoghurt or liqueur-flavoured cream.

For first-time tasters, if the fruit appears too rich in flavour, combine it with a cream base, such as in a soufflé or ice cream. The tangy tamarillo complements many rich foods.

It is delicious in pies and cheesecakes and puréed and sweetened it makes a super sauce for iced desserts or pancakes.

The tamarillo blends well with other fruits too. If preparing a red tamarillo salad in advance, choose other red fruits to serve with it. For example, red currants or blackberries. Otherwise, add the tamarillo to the salad just before serving to prevent its bright red colour from spreading.

The golden fruit is more apricot in flavour and combines with all other fruits readily. Purées of the two tamarillos, provide easy sauces to complement plain desserts. These can be flavoured with liqueurs if desired. For example, 'individual steamed puddings with two coloured sauces' — the purées can be spooned either side of the little puddings. Hot or cold, tamarillo desserts are favourites the world over.

Rolled Tamarillo Pavlova

A dessert meringue is rolled around a filling of tamarillo and cream.

6 egg whites
1½ cups sugar
1 teaspoon vanilla
1 teaspoon vinegar
1 tablespoon cornflour (cornstarch)
1½ cups cream
3 tablespoons icing (confectioners') sugar
2 tamarillos, peeled and puréed
1 tablespoon sugar
extra icing (confectioners') sugar

Beat egg whites until stiff. Gradually add sugar, beating well until all sugar is dissolved. Fold in vanilla, vinegar and cornflour.

Spread evenly into a greased and lined 28 × 35 cm (11 × 14 in) lamington tray.

Bake at 180°C (350°F) for 15 minutes, until lightly golden.

Sprinkle a piece of greaseproof with extra icing sugar. When meringue is cooked, turn onto the paper. Cool.

Whip cream with 3 tablespoons icing sugar. Fold in puréed fruit combined with the tablespoon of sugar. Spread over the pavlova and roll up along the long edge, using the edge of the paper to help roll the pavlova. Use a long spatula to place the roll onto a serving dish. Dust with extra icing sugar. Serves about 10.

Gateau Verand

(See photograph, page 37)

Cake
3 eggs
½ cup castor (powdered) sugar
¾ cup self-raising flour
1 teaspoon butter
2 tablespoons hot water

Filling
1 cup cottage cheese
½ cup cream, whipped
3 tablespoons orange liqueur

Topping
3 red tamarillos
2-3 golden tamarillos
red currant jelly

Case
150 g (5 oz) dark chocolate
1 teaspoon vegetable
shortening

To make cake, beat eggs until light and thick. Gradually beat in the sugar until it is completely dissolved. Sift flour several times. Melt butter in the hot water. Sift flour into the egg mixture and fold in with water. Pour into a greased and lightly floured 20 cm (8 in) square cake pan. Bake 180°C (350°F) for 20-25 minutes. Turn onto a cake cooler. When cold, split in half through the centre.

Beat cottage cheese until creamy. Add half the cream and the liqueur. Spread over the base half of the cake. Place other half on top.

Peel and slice tamarillos. Place red and golden tamarillos in alternate lines to cover the cake. Warm the jelly, mix until smooth and spoon over the fruit. Refrigerate.

Break chocolate into squares. Melt with vegetable shortening, mixing until smooth and shiny. Cool a little, then pour onto waxed paper. Refrigerate until set. Cut into straight strips about 4 cm (1½ in) wide and 20 cm (8 in) long. Spread remaining cream around the outside of the cake and press the strips of chocolate onto each side. Serves 6-8.

Cheesecake Gold

Base
250 g (9 oz) digestive biscuits
1 teaspoon ground cinnamon
1 teaspoon ground nutmeg
100 g (3½ oz) butter, melted

Filling
3 large golden tamarillos
2 tablespoons sugar
2 eggs
⅔ cup sugar
1 tablespoon powdered gelatine
2 tablespoons lemon juice
350 g (12 oz) cottage cheese
300 ml (10½ fl oz) cream, whipped
½ cup chopped crystallised ginger

Glaze
2 golden tamarillos
½ teaspoon gelatine
¼ cup water
¼ cup orange juice

Crush biscuits finely and combine with spices and butter. Press into the base of a greased, 20 cm (8 in) cake pan with a loose base. Chill.

To prepare filling, peel and slice tamarillos. Place in a small heavy pan with the 2 tablespoons sugar and simmer gently until cooked. Purée and sieve.

Separate 1 egg and reserve the white. Place remaining egg and yolk into the top of a double boiler with the ⅔ cup sugar. Beat well over hot water until thick and smooth.

Soak gelatine in juice, dissolve over hot water and add to the tamarillos. Beat cottage cheese until smooth, sieve if required. Fold egg and tamarillo mixtures into the cottage cheese with chopped ginger. Whip egg white and fold with cream into cheese. Pour into cake pan and refrigerate to set.

To prepare glaze, peel and slice tamarillos and place on top of cheesecake. Soak gelatine in water, add strained juice and dissolve over hot water. When cool, spoon over the cake. Refrigerate to set. Serves 8.

Pink Soufflé with Grapes

Soufflé
400 g (14 oz) red tamarillos
1 tablespoon powdered gelatine
¼ cup water
3 eggs, separated
½ cup castor (powdered) sugar
¾ cup cream, lightly whipped
2 tablespoons extra castor (powdered) sugar

Filling
500 g (1 lb) green and purple skinned grapes

Prepare a 15 cm (6 in) soufflé dish, tie a band of double greaseproof paper around the outside of the dish, to extend about 5 cm (2 in) above the top of the dish.

Peel tamarillos, reserving a few slices for decoration. Purée remainder in a food processor or blender.

Soften gelatine in the water. Dissolve over hot water and stir into the purée.

Beat egg yolks and half cup of castor sugar until thick. Fold in tamarillo purée. Beat egg whites and 2 tablespoons castor sugar until stiff. Gradually combine tamarillo mixture with cream. Fold in egg whites.

Remove any stalks from the grapes and mix to combine the two colours. Scatter half the filling over the base of the soufflé dish. Cover with half the soufflé mixture. Repeat layers. Refrigerate until set.

Decorate with a few slices of tamarillo and a few small flowers and their leaves. Serves 8.

Yoghurt Tamarillo Creams

Use golden or red tamarillos.

4 tamarillos, peeled and puréed
¾ cup plain yoghurt
5 tablespoons icing (confectioners') sugar
1 tablespoon powdered gelatine
juice of ½ an orange
¾ cup cream, whipped
mint leaves

Combine half the tamarillo purée with the yoghurt and sugar. Soften the gelatine in the orange juice then dissolve over hot water. Stir into the tamarillo mixture. Chill for 5 minutes.

Fold in stiffly whipped cream then divide the mixture into 6 small individual moulds. Refrigerate to set for 3 or 4 hours.

Dip moulds into warm water then unmould onto 6 serving plates. Sweeten remaining purée if required then place 2 spoonfuls onto each plate. Garnish with mint leaves. Serves 6.

Quick Kirsch Dessert

Peel and slice 4 tamarillos and sprinkle with 2 tablespoons each castor (powdered) sugar and Kirsch. Cover and stand several hours. Make up a strawberry jelly using 1¼ cups boiling water. Cool. Whip 1 cup cream and fold into jelly with tamarillos. Pour into a mould and set. Serves 4-6.

Tamarillo Fruit Salads

Tamarillos combine well with other interesting fruits to produce exotic dessert salads.

- tamarillos and blueberries sweetened with maple syrup and topped with long thread coconut

- blackberries, apples and tamarillos with crème de cassis

- tamarillos soaked in strawberry liqueur, tossed with watermelon balls and served from the melon

- tamarillos and kiwifruit layered alternately in a bowl, and sprinkled with sugar

- feijoas and tamarillos sliced, sweetened and topped with toasted chopped pecans

- raspberries, honeydew melon and tamarillos sprinkled with Cointreau.

Family's Favourite

A simple combination of peeled and sliced red tamarillos sprinkled with white or brown sugar. To every 500 g (1 lb) fruit allow 3-4 tablespoons sugar depending on taste. Stand covered for several hours in the refrigerator for juices to develop. Serve any time of the day.

Golden Chocolate Dippers

Choose bitter or semi-sweet chocolate for coating the tamarillos. (See photograph, page 45)

6 golden tamarillos
½ cup water
¼ cup sugar
2 tablespoons orange flavoured liqueur
200 g (7 oz) dark, bitter chocolate
1 teaspoon vegetable shortening

Peel tamarillos leaving stalks attached. Heat water in a saucepan and dissolve the sugar. Add the tamarillos and poach over low heat for 10 minutes, until just cooked. Remove from the heat and add liqueur. Cool. Remove tamarillos from liquid and pat dry with paper towels.

Break chocolate into pieces and place in a small bowl with vegetable shortening. Melt over hot water or in microwave oven about 1½ minutes. Stir well until shiny.

Carefully dip tamarillos in, one at a time, so the chocolate covers about half the fruit. Spread evenly with a knife. Place on chilled foil and refrigerate until set. These may be prepared up to 4 hours before being served. Good with plain yoghurt. Serves 6.

Poached in Red Wine

(Cover photograph)

Combine 1 cup sugar, 1 cup red wine and ½ cup water in a wide pan. Simmer for 4 minutes, stirring to dissolve the sugar. Add 8 tamarillos to the pan, leaving skins on and stalks attached. Poach for about 10 minutes. Remove tamarillos from the syrup and remove skins by cutting carefully around the stem end with sharp scissors. Return to the pan to cool. Refrigerate. Serve with sour cream and a little juice, or drain and serve in brandy snap baskets, and top with liquid honey. Serves 4.

Tamarillo Phyllo Pie

A crisp phyllo pastry shell is filled with cherry-flavoured cream and topped with tamarillos.

Pie shell
8 sheets phyllo pastry
50 g (2 oz) butter, melted

Filling
1½ cups cream, whipped
1 teaspoon powdered gelatine
2 tablespoons water
2 tablespoons Kirsch or Cherry Brandy

Topping
2 tamarillos
tamarillo or red currant jelly
icing (confectioners') sugar

Trim sheets of phyllo roughly to fit a 20-23 cm (8-9 in) flan tin, allowing pastry to come up the sides.

Lightly grease the flan tin. Brush one sheet of phyllo with a little butter and line into the tin. Repeat with the remaining phyllo. Lightly press a sheet of foil onto the top pastry layer. Bake 200°C (400°F) for 5 minutes, remove foil and continue baking 4-5 minutes until golden. Cool.

Soak gelatine in cold water until swollen. Dissolve over hot water. Cool then fold into the whipped cream with the flavouring. Spoon into the cooled pie shell and refrigerate until set.

Peel and slice tamarillos. Place on the filling and brush with warmed jelly. Dust with icing sugar just before serving. Serves about 6.

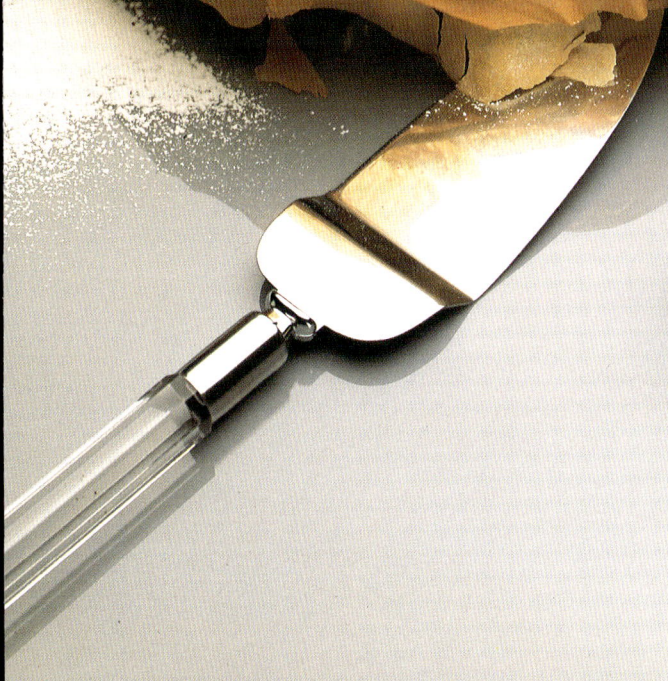

Tamarillo Strudel

2 cooking apples
6 large tamarillos
¼ cup sugar
½ cup raisins

Crumb mixture
½ cup dried breadcrumbs
¼ cup each, ground almonds, sugar
¼ teaspoon each, ground nutmeg, cinnamon

8 sheets phyllo pastry
150 g (5 oz) butter

Peel apples and slice into a saucepan. Add 2 tablespoons water and cook on low heat until softened. Add peeled and sliced tamarillos and sugar, and cook until soft and liquid is reduced. Add raisins and cool.

Combine all ingredients for crumb mixture. Layer 2 sheets of phyllo on a flat surface. Brush lightly with butter and sprinkle with 3 tablespoons of the crumb mixture. Continue layering 2 sheets of phyllo on top, brushing with butter and sprinkling with crumbs, three more times. Spoon filling over top of pastry. Fold in ends 2 cm (¾ in), then roll up swiss roll fashion.

Place seam side down on a lightly greased baking tray, brush with butter and bake 45 minutes at 180°C (350°F) until golden. Cool slightly before serving. Dust with icing sugar. Serves about 8.

Crisp Tamarillo Rolls

Lay a sheet of phyllo out on a flat surface and brush lightly with melted butter. Top with another sheet. Place a peeled tamarillo in the centre at one end of the phyllo. Sprinkle with a tablespoon of brown sugar and a dash of cinnamon. Fold over sides to enclose the tamarillo and roll up. Place on a lightly greased oven tray and brush with butter. Repeat to make as many rolls as required. Bake 180°C (350°F) for about 25 minutes until golden. Serve one per person.

Tamarillo Tartin

A variation of the famous upside-down apple tartin

Pastry
1 ¼ cups flour
⅛ teaspoon salt
1 ½ tablespoons castor (powdered) sugar
125 g (4 oz) chilled butter
4-5 tablespoons icy water

Filling
8 tamarillos
¼ cup sugar
1 teaspoon cinnamon
25 g (1 oz) softened unsalted butter
¼ cup sugar, extra
50 g (2 oz) unsalted butter, melted

Prepare pastry first. Sift flour and salt into a bowl or food processor. Add sugar. Dice the butter and rub in until mixture resembles breadcrumbs. Add enough water, a little at a time, to make a stiff dough. Wrap in waxed paper and refrigerate at least 1 hour before using.

Peel tamarillos and cut in halves lengthwise. Sprinkle with sugar and cinnamon.

Grease a 20-23 cm (8-9 in) baking pan well, with the softened butter. Sprinkle half the extra sugar over the base then top with the tamarillos, placing the cut side down. Sprinkle with melted butter and remaining sugar.

Roll out pastry to about 5 mm (¼ in) thick. Cut into a circle the same diameter as the pan. Place over the tamarillos, allowing its edges to fall against the inside edge of the pan. Cut 4 holes in the top of the pastry to allow the steam to escape.

Bake in the lower part of the oven, 190°C (375°F) for 45-60 minutes. Unmould tart onto a serving dish. Serve warm with whipped or sour cream. Serves 6-8.

Tamarillo Winter Sponge

6 tamarillos
2 tablespoons brown sugar

Sponge topping
125 g (4 oz) butter
½ cup sugar
1 egg
1 cup flour
1½ teaspoons baking powder
icing (confectioners') sugar

Peel tamarillos and slice into the base of the deep pie dish. Sprinkle with brown sugar. Place in oven at 190°C (375°F) for 15 minutes, until cooked and hot.

Meanwhile, beat butter and sugar until light. Add egg, beating well. Sift in flour and baking powder. Mix carefully. Pour over hot fruit and continue baking at the same temperature for about 45 minutes.

Sprinkle with icing sugar and serve immediately. Serves 4-6.

Individual Alaskas

Cut 4 thick squares of sponge cake and sprinkle with port. Top each square with a peeled, poached tamarillo. Sprinkle with a little sugar. Place on suitable serving plates. Beat 2 egg whites until stiff and fold in ¼ cup castor (powdered) sugar, beating until shiny. Cover tamarillos with the meringue. Place under a hot grill until golden. Pour over some warmed brandy and ignite.

Clafouti with Tamarillo

A batter hides the fruit while it is baking. A simple dessert to make.

1 ¼ cups milk
¼ cup sugar
3 eggs
1 tablespoon vanilla
¾ cup flour
4-5 tamarillos
¼ cup sugar, extra
icing (confectioners') sugar
½ cup flaked almonds, optional

Place milk, sugar, eggs, vanilla and flour into a food processor or blender and mix until smooth.

Peel and slice tamarillos thickly.

Pour a thin layer of batter, about 5 mm (¼ in), into a deep pie dish or baking pan. Place in the oven 180°C (350°F) until it sets. Remove from oven and spread with tamarillos.

Sprinkle with extra sugar and pour over remaining batter. Continue baking for about 1 hour. Serve hot, dusted with icing sugar and flaked almonds. Serves about 6.

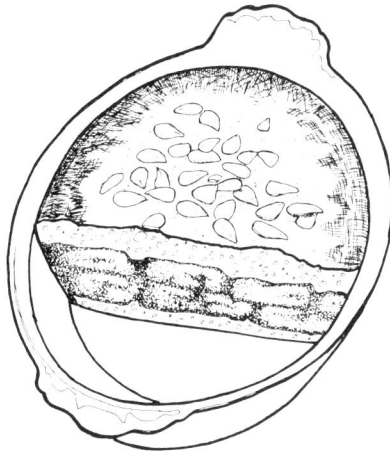

Crêpes Mont d'Or

Crêpes
6 tablespoons flour
¼ teaspoon salt
2 teaspoons sugar
2 eggs
¾ cup milk
1 tablespoon oil
butter or oil for frying

Filling
6 tamarillos
4 tablespoons raw sugar
2 tablespoons Cognac
75 g (3 oz) toasted hazelnuts
icing (confectioners') sugar
whipped or sour cream

To make the crêpes, sift dry ingredients into a bowl. Beat eggs, add to dry ingredients. Mix in milk and oil. Stand for 2 hours.

Heat a small heavy frypan, swirl a little butter or oil over the surface. Spoon 2-3 tablespoons batter into the pan, swirling mixture to cover the pan. Cook until golden, about 1 minute each side.

Repeat until all mixture is used, stacking the crêpes as they are cooled. Makes about 12.

To prepare the filling, peel and dice the tamarillos. Sprinkle with sugar and Cognac and stand for an hour for juices to develop. Just before serving heat until warm.

Place 2 crêpes on each plate. Spoon a little of the fruit mixture into each crêpe, top with nuts, and fold over. Dust with icing sugar and serve with whipped or sour cream. Serves 6.

Tamarillo Crunch

500 g (1 lb) tamarillos, peeled
1 tablespoon custard powder
1 tablespoon brown sugar
1 cup rolled oats
½ cup wholemeal flour
1 cup brown sugar
125 g (4 oz) butter

Slice tamarillos and sprinkle with custard powder and tablespoon of brown sugar.

Combine rolled oats, flour and sugar in a bowl and rub in butter until mixture is crumbly. Place half the oat mixture on the base of a greased 20 cm (8 in) pie dish, pressing down firmly. Cover with the tamarillo mixture, and top with remaining oat mixture. Bake 45 minutes at 180°C (350°F). Serve warm with cream or ice cream. Serves 6.

Flamed Tamarillos

Peel 6 or 8 tamarillos and remove stems. Melt 25 g (1 oz) butter in a chafing dish and add the juice of 1 orange and 1 lemon. Stir and heat until smooth. Add the fruit and sprinkle with 3 tablespoons raw sugar. Turn fruit carefully, cooking until just cooked on the outside. Warm some cognac or brandy, pour over the fruit and flame. These could be served with folded crêpes, or lightly whipped cream and sprinkled with chopped pistachio nuts.

Tamarillo and Pistachio Nut Ice Cream

The red tamarillos are complemented by the green pistachio nuts.

5 red tamarillos
¼ cup castor (powdered) sugar
2 teaspoons powdered gelatine
2 tablespoons water
75 g (3 oz) pistachio nuts
1¼ cups cream, whipped
2 tablespoons castor (powdered) sugar

Peel and slice tamarillos into a saucepan. Sprinkle the ¼ cup castor sugar over the fruit and stand for 15 minutes. Bring to the boil and cook 1 minute.

Purée in a food processor or blender. Sieve to remove the seeds.

Soften the powdered gelatine in water. Dissolve over hot water. Add to purée. Cool.

Remove shells from pistachios and place the nuts into a small bowl. Pour boiling water over to cover and soak for 1 minute. Drain and refresh in icy water. Remove skins and pat dry.

Combine whipped cream and the 2 tablespoons castor sugar. Fold into the purée with the nuts. Freeze until almost set, beat until light, then freeze until firm. Serves 4.

Ginger Gold Ice Cream

See photograph page 53.

6 golden tamarillos
¾ cup castor (powdered) sugar
⅓ cup diced stem ginger in syrup
2 tablespoons ginger syrup
3 eggs, separated
1¼ cups cream, whipped

Peel tamarillos then purée in a blender or food processor. Add sugar and stir to dissolve. Add ginger and syrup.

Beat egg yolks over hot water until thickened and creamy. Cool.

Beat egg whites until stiff. Fold yolks, whites and cream into the fruit. Freeze until mushy, beat well, then freeze until solid. Serves 4.

Quick Tamarillo Ice Cream

Purée or chop 3 peeled tamarillos and add 2 tablespoons sugar. Allow 500 ml (1 pint) vanilla or strawberry ice cream to soften slightly. Fold in purée and refreeze.

Superb Sauce for Ice Cream

Peel 4 tamarillos and place in a blender. Add ¼ cup sugar and purée until smooth. Pour over ice cream in a tall glass. This sauce may be kept refrigerated for 3-4 days or it may be frozen. Makes about 1¼ cups, enough for 4 servings.

Tamarillo Sorbet

Serve as a palate refresher between courses or as a dessert with lightly whipped cream. (Photograph page 53.)

1.5 kg (3 lb) red tamarillos
1 tablespoon lemon juice
4 teaspoons powdered gelatine
½ cup water
juice of 1 lemon
3½ cups water
1½ cups sugar
3 eggs whites

Peel the tamarillos. Purée in a food processor or blender. Sieve to remove the seeds. Add lemon juice.

Soak gelatine in ½ cup water. Boil the second measure of water and sugar for 10 minutes. Add gelatine and dissolve. Cool and add purée. Chill in refrigerator.

Whip egg whites until stiff. Fold into purée mixture and freeze in a covered container. Serves 8-10.

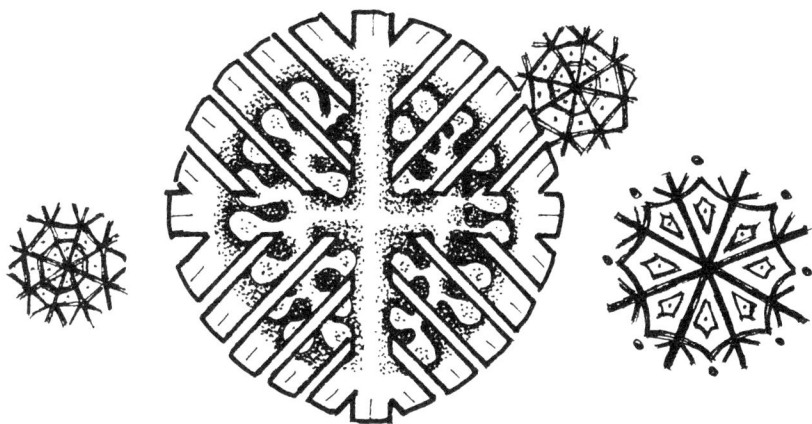

Tamarillo Lunchbox Cake

6 red tamarillos
2 teaspoons baking soda
125 g (4 oz) butter
1 cup sugar
2 tablespoons cocoa
½ teaspoon mixed spice
½ teaspoon cinnamon
2 cups flour
1 teaspoon cream of tartar
1 cup raisins

Peel tamarillos and poach in ½ cup water for about 5 minutes until just tender. Drain and dice fruit. Dissolve 1½ teaspoons soda in the warm tamarillos.

Cream butter and sugar until light. Sift dry ingredients plus remaining soda. Add tamarillos to butter mixture alternately with dry ingredients. Stir in raisins. Pour into a greased and floured 20 cm (8 in) cake pan. Bake 180°C (350°F) for about 45 minutes. Allow to cool in the pan. Ice with butter icing if required.

Golden Muffins

4 cups flour
1 teaspoon salt
1 tablespoon baking powder
⅓ cup raw sugar
3 golden tamarillos, peeled and diced
1¼ cups milk, approximately
¼ cup soy bean oil
2 eggs, lightly beaten

Sift flour, salt and baking powder into a bowl. Sprinkle sugar over the tamarillos in another bowl. Combine with the milk, oil and eggs, and stir into the flour mixture. Mix until just moistened. Spoon into lightly greased muffin tins, about ⅔ full. Bake 200°C (400°F) for about 25 minutes until golden. Makes about 12 muffins.

PRESERVES

Freezing is a quick, easy and efficient method of preserving tamarillos.

Select mature fruit free from blemishes. Frozen tamarillos keep in good condition for 12 months.

a) Peel fruit and slice into a bowl. Sprinkle with ¼ cup white or brown sugar for every 500 g (1 lb) fruit. Stand for 2-3 hours for juices to develop. Pour into a suitable container for freezing. To use, merely thaw the fruit and serve.

Golden tamarillos may benefit from the addition of ½ teaspoon ascorbic acid powder to keep them a great golden colour.

b) Peel and purée the fruit, adding sugar to taste. Sieve to remove seeds if desired. Pour into rigid containers to freeze. If preferred, the tamarillos could be cooked prior to puréeing but the raw purée has a better colour. Use for sauces, drinks, toppings, or incorporate into recipes.

c) Whole fruit may be frozen 'as is'. This fruit is good for cooked dishes. The skin can be removed before freezing if preferred.

d) Slices can be frozen by the free-flow method. Place in a single layer on a tray and freeze until solid. Remove from tray and pack into airtight containers. Use the slices for tarts or pies, or in salads.

Red Tamarillo Jam

This jam may also be prepared in the microwave. Divide recipe in half if necessary. Follow instructions up to the cooking. Cook about 7 minutes or until setting point is reached.

2 kg (4 lb) red tamarillos
2 kg (4 lb) sugar
juice of 2 lemons
2 cups boiling water

Pour boiling water over the tamarillos and stand for 2-3 minutes. Refresh in cold water then peel.

Slice thickly, place in a bowl and sprinkle with half the sugar and the juice of the lemons. Stand overnight.

Next day bring to the boil, add remaining sugar and the 2 cups boiling water. Boil for about 25 minutes, until setting point is reached, 104°C (220°F). Pour into hot clean jars and cover.

Golden Tamarillo and Apricot Jam

This jam has a beautiful colour.

500 g (1 lb) dried apricots
5 cups water
500 g (1 lb) golden tamarillos
7 cups sugar

Chop apricots and place in a bowl. Pour water over and soak for 24 hours.

Peel tamarillos and slice thickly. Add to apricots in a saucepan and boil until tender. Add sugar and simmer about 30 minutes until setting point is reached, 104°C (220°F). Stir occasionally. Pour into sterilised jars. Cover.

Tamarillo Jelly

Use firm, just-ripe fruit for this jelly. Substitute 1 tart apple for a tamarillo if pectin content is in doubt.

1 kg (2 lb) red tamarillos
1 lemon, sliced
1 litre (quart) water
sugar

Peel tamarillos and chop fruit. Place in a large saucepan with the sliced lemon. Add water and boil for 20 minutes.

Pour mixture into a jelly bag and strain overnight. Do not squeeze or jelly will go cloudy. Next day, measure the liquid. Add ¾ cup sugar for each cup of tamarillo juice. Bring to boiling point, stirring until sugar is dissolved, then boil for about 30 minutes until setting point is reached. Remove from heat and stand 5 minutes, then pour into hot sterilised jars. Seal when cold.

Tamarillos Preserved in Red Wine

Red tamarillos are used in this preserve. Golden tamarillos could be preserved in sauterne, or use a medium syrup.

2 cups good red wine
½ cup sugar
1 kg (2 lb) tamarillos

Method One. Bring wine to the boil and dissolve the sugar in it. Peel tamarillos, halve if very large and poach in the liquid until just cooked. Spoon fruit into clean preserving jars and fill to overflowing with the boiling liquid. Seal with a vacuum seal.
Method Two. The peeled, uncooked fruit can also be placed in jars and the boiling liquid poured over. The jars and fruit can be placed into the microwave oven and cooked for 4 minutes on high, or in the conventional oven at 150°C (300°F) for about 30 minutes. Remove jars, top up with a little boiling syrup and seal.

Tamarillo Sauce

A great sauce for barbecues or use in Oriental cooking in place of Chinese plum sauce.

3.5 kg (7 lb) tamarillos, peeled and sliced
1 kg (2 lb) apples, peeled and sliced
3 onions, chopped
1 litre (quart) vinegar
2 tablespoons salt
4 cups sugar
½ teaspoon cayenne (optional)
1 tablespoon finely chopped root ginger
1 teaspoon each whole peppercorns, cloves, allspice berries

Place prepared fruits and vegetables into a large pan with vinegar, salt, sugar and spices tied in muslin. Simmer over low heat until very soft, about 2 hours.

Remove spices. Purée in a blender or food processor or pass through a sieve. Return to a clean pan and simmer until thick, about 45 minutes. Pour into hot clean bottles. Seal when cold. The tops can be dipped into melted wax for an airtight seal. Makes about 2 litres.

Pickled Tamarillos

Serve with meats or cheeses.

1 kg (2 lb) tamarillos
1½ cups sugar
1 cup cider vinegar
2 cinnamon sticks

Blanch and peel tamarillos. Slice fruit or cut in halves. Dissolve sugar in hot vinegar and simmer with cinnamon sticks for 10 minutes. Add tamarillos and poach for about 5 minutes. Spoon hot fruit into clean sterilised jars and fill to overflowing with hot liquid. Seal with vacuum seals. Keep for at least 4 weeks before using.

Refrigerator Relish

4 large tamarillos
1 green-skinned apple, diced
1 onion, peeled and diced
2 stalks celery, diced
1 carrot, shredded
1 green pepper, diced
1 clove garlic, crushed
1 teaspoon salt
1 tablespoon prepared horseradish
¼ cup sugar
3 tablespoons cider vinegar

Peel and slice the tamarillos into a saucepan.

Add all other ingredients to pan. Bring to boiling point, stirring. Serve warm or pour into jars, cover and refrigerate for up to 2 weeks. Serve with cold meats or grills, or use as a filling for pita bread. Makes about 500 ml (1 pint).

Traditional Tamarillo Relish

2.5 kg (5 lb) red tamarillos
500 g (1 lb) onions
500 g (1 lb) apples
500 g (1 lb) brown sugar
750 ml (1½ pints) vinegar
1 teaspoon mixed spice
1 teaspoon curry powder
½ teaspoon salt

Blanch and peel tamarillos. Chop and place in a saucepan with diced onions and apples and all remaining ingredients. Stir well. Bring to the boil and simmer 2 hours until thick. Allow to go cold before storing in sterilised jars and sealing. Makes about 2 kg (4 lb).

Tamarillo Vinegar

Delicious used in salad dressings or spooned over chicken or game.

500 g (1 lb) red tamarillos
2 cups red wine vinegar
sugar

Peel and chop tamarillos into a glass or ceramic bowl. Cover with the vinegar. Cover and stand for 3 days, stirring occasionally.

Strain and measure the liquid. Add 1½ cups sugar to each 2½ cups of liquid.

Bring to the boil, stirring to dissolve the sugar. Simmer 10 minutes. Pour into sterilised bottles and seal. Makes about 500 ml (1 pint).

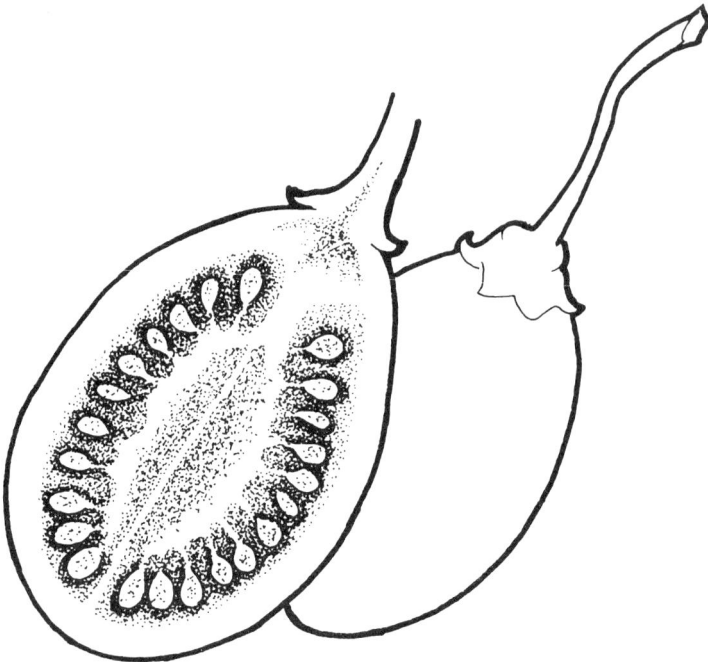

INDEX